THE
Mennonite
Starter Kit

THE Mennonite Starter Kit

CRAIG HAAS
STEVE NOLT

Good Books

Intercourse, PA 17534

Photography Credits

Andrews Photography (Courtesy of Bluffton College)-79; Harold S. Bender Collection, Archives of the Mennonite Church-75; Associated Mennonite Biblical Seminaries (AMBS)/Mark Boyce-73; AMBS/Steve Echols-75; Jonathan Charles-77; Conrad Grebel College-73; Eastern Mennonite College and Seminary (EMC&S-20, 73); EMC/Jim Bishop-20; James Ewing-56; *Festival Quarterly*/Merle Good-31; Good Books/Merle Good-75; Good Books/Kenneth Pellman-25, 89; Good Books/Dawn Ranck-32, 75, 87; Good Books/Stephen Scott-26, 50, 51; Herald Press-77, 79; John P. Herr-61; Tyler Klassen-13; Mennonite Central Committee/Jim King-15; Mennonite Your Way-48; The People's Place-44, 63, 75; Arlie J. Regier-15; Menno Simons Historical Library & Archives at EMC&S-73.

Drawings on pages 6, 18-19, 37, 42, 55, and 67 by Cheryl Benner.

Artwork on cover and pages 16, 26, 32, 60-61, 68, 71, 77, and 87 designed by Craig Haas.

"Modern Day Menno Sightings Continue" first appeared as a column by Steve Nolt in the *Goshen College Record* in November, 1989. It is included here in an adapted form.

Design by Dawn J. Ranck

The Mennonite Starter Kit
Copyright © 1993 by Good Books, Intercourse, PA 17534
International Standard Book Number: 1-56148-085-1
Library of Congress Card Catalog Number: 93-24215

Library of Congress Cataloging-in-Publication Data

Haas, J. Craig, 1956-
    The Mennonite starter kit / Craig Haas, Steve Nolt.
        p. cm.
    ISBN 1-56148-085-1 (pbk.) : $5.95
    1. Mennonites—Humor. 2. Mennonites—Membership. I. Nolt, Steven M., 1968- . II. Title.
BX8121.2.H32 1993
289.7—dc20   93-24215
                                                                  CIP

Table of Contents

Dear New Mennonite:

(DON'T TURN THAT PAGE!)

You've just discovered how very easy it is to join a Mennonite church these days, and you'll soon discover just how hard it is to really become a Mennonite.

To really *be* a Mennonite, it's essential that you learn the habits and symbols—and Mennonite symbols aren't as obvious as they used to be. In a way it's now more difficult to don a Mennonite identity than it was when many Mennonites wore their identity on their sleeves—and in other apparel as well.

Today's symbols are the shifting rules and unspoken attitudes, loyalties, and preferences, which are just as important for us Mennonites now, as Low German or plain clothing were a generation or two ago. These less visible symbols can be confusing and even disconcerting to the uninitiated. Likewise, jargon and name-dropping can baffle and confound the novice in search of a Mennonite identity. Today more than ever, we Mennonites in North America might *look* like our non-Mennonite neighbors, and even *believe* the same things they do, but this doesn't make us any less a "peculiar people." We keep finding new ways.

Unfortunately for many New Mennonites, no one ever passes on this vital inside information. The unwritten but assumed requirements for acceptance in the real Mennonite world seldom find verbal expression. Church membership classes consist almost entirely of lessons on Mennonite doctrine with a dash of church history tossed in on occasion. New Mennonites are left to discover alone the many habits and assumptions of their new family of faith. In this handy volume we provide you with a guide to everything you need to know about Mennonites but weren't taught in church membership class.

We wish to thank the following staff members of the People's Place who offered their suggestions, evaluations, and sometimes their material, and who are thereby partly to blame for this book: Cheryl Benner, Norma Gehman, Merle Good, Phyllis Good, Sharon Kraybill, Dean Mast, Jan Mast, Kenny Pellman, Rachel Pellman, Dawn Ranck, Steve Scott, Louise Stoltzfus, and Elizabeth Weaver Kreider.

As a New Mennonite you'll have to begin taking yourself too seriously; but please, don't take *us* too seriously!

Craig Haas and Steve Nolt

1.
Peoplehood
and Heritage

We begin with perhaps the most enigmatic aspect of being a Mennonite today—the twins Peoplehood and Heritage. For as hard as many Mennonites try to look, think, and act like their non-Mennonite neighbors, there are some things that remain very much intact. Ethnic backgrounds and folk legends live on, an assumed part of church life. Subtle group hopes, preferences, and fears continue. As a New Mennonite, the material in this section will help you understand your new church family—and help explain why they have so much difficulty understanding you.

In this section you will learn . . .

. . . the differences between Russian Mennonites and Swiss Mennonites.

. . . about non-Mennonites whom Mennonites wish were Mennonite.

. . . why some people believe that Menno Simons is alive and living with Elvis.

. . . about the church's overwhelming preoccupation with "Mennonite Identity."

You're Really a Mennonite When . . .

. . . you know how other people's out-of-state relatives are related to each other.

. . . someone sneezes and you say "Gelassenheit."

. . . you have a relative named Esther.

. . . you can trace your family tree at least six ways to the same immigrant.

. . . you feel compelled to explain to others that you're not Amish.

. . . it *is* necessary to explain that you're not Mormon.

. . . you know that Anabaptist was not the wife of John the Baptist.

. . . your parents aren't Muslim, but they named you Omar.

. . . you think that a book describing 4,000 grisly executions might make a nice wedding gift.

Little-known Facts
and Statistics about Mennonites
(Source: *Mennonite Mosaic—The Missing Tiles*, 1992)

☺   Most of today's Russian Mennonites never lived in Russia and don't know a word of Russian.

☺   Of American men who still wear sideburns, 84% are Mennonite pastors from the Midwest; 17% are Elvis impersonators.

☺   One percent of Amish men say that it is wrong for a Christian to fight in war. The rest could not be reached by phone.

☺   There are more Lapps in Mennonite church leadership than in all of Finland.

☺   Ninety-two percent of Canadian Mennonites believe that Winnipeg, Manitoba, is the largest Mennonite community in the world. Ninety-four percent of Mennonites in Lancaster, Pennsylvania, believe that Winnipeg is the largest Mennonite community in Canada.

☺   Three-fourths of Mennonites say that it is wrong to use alcohol; the other quarter say it depends on what you use it for.

☺   Fifteen percent of Canadian Mennonites suffer from some degree of chronic Winnipegosis.

☺   Sixty-five percent of all Mennonites think that war has its disadvantages.

☺ Eighty percent of American Mennonites mistakenly believe that Toronto is the capital of Canada. Twenty-one percent of Canadian Mennonites mistakenly believe that Newton, Kansas, is the capital of the United States.

☺ Prior to a Mennonite college's first authorized dance, 15% of the student body believed that Mennonites shouldn't dance. Afterwards, the feeling was unanimous.

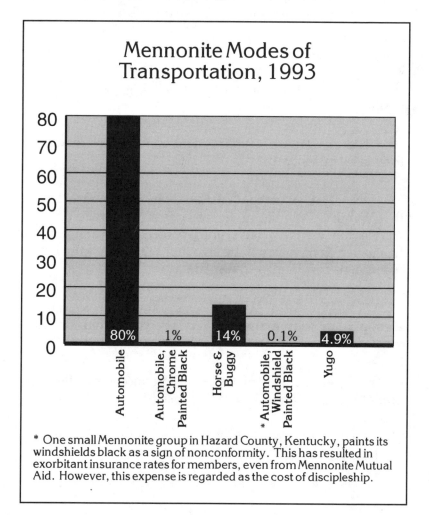

Mennonite Modes of Transportation, 1993

* One small Mennonite group in Hazard County, Kentucky, paints its windshields black as a sign of nonconformity. This has resulted in exorbitant insurance rates for members, even from Mennonite Mutual Aid. However, this expense is regarded as the cost of discipleship.

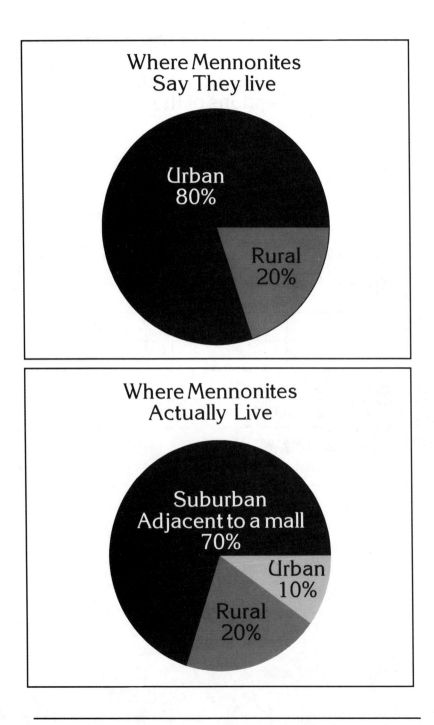

Where Mennonites
Say They live

Urban
80%

Rural
20%

Where Mennonites
Actually Live

Suburban
Adjacent to a mall
70%

Urban
10%

Rural
20%

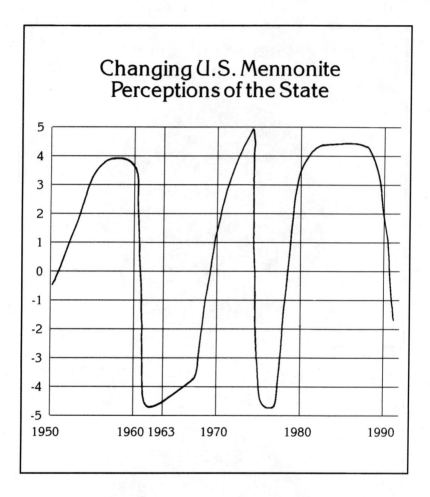

Changing U.S. Mennonite
Perceptions of the State

A Tale of Two Mennonite Cultures

Today's Mennonites are experiencing more ethnic diversity than in the past. However, two great ethnic streams continue to dominate the Mennonite landscape: the "Russian" Mennonites whose Dutch ancestors migrated to Prussia, then to Russia, then to North and South Americas; and the "Swiss" Mennonites whose ancestors came to the U.S. from Switzerland and southern Germany and spread into Canada. To acquaint New Mennonites with each of these older types, we present the following guide.

Russian Mennonites:	**Swiss Mennonites:**
☞ sometimes speak Low German.	☞ sometimes speak Pennsylvania Dutch.
☞ eat zwieback with borscht.	☞ eat pretzels and pig stomach.
☞ believe Menno started the Mennonites.	☞ know Conrad Grebel did.
☞ can't forget Russia.	☞ can't remember Switzerland.
☞ don't know any Amish.	☞ don't know any Hutterites.
☞ are trying to understand themselves.	☞ are trying to understand Russian Mennonites.
☞ have German names like Heinrich and Werner.	☞ have German names like Raymond and Lester.
☞ are plains people.	☞ are plain people. *(You saw that one coming!)*
☞ sometimes fled to South America to avoid Communism.	☞ sometimes fled to Central America to avoid liberalism.
☞ write vivid disturbing poetry.	☞ don't.

Non-Mennonites Whom Mennonites Wish Were Mennonite

From time to time someone comes along who captures the imagination of Mennonites better than most other Mennonites can. Sometimes we wonder whether they have been influenced by Mennonites. Some of them seem to speak and act as if they were Mennonite. Maybe they become our heroes because they exemplify Mennonite values. Or maybe we envy their popularity for doing the things that we do. Or possibly we just can't help liking them too much for our own good. In any case, as a New Mennonite you'll be finding these folks talked about and admired a great deal in Mennonite circles.

Garrison Keillor

Tony Campolo

Alice Parker

Jimmy Carter

Henri Nouwen

Mark Hatfield

Lloyd Bentsen
  (but he's no Mark Hatfield!)

Garrison Keillor

P. Buckley Moss

Paul Stookey

Mother Teresa

Rembrandt

Judy Collins

Stanley Hauerwas

Garrison Keillor

Thomas Muentzer

Ronald Reagan

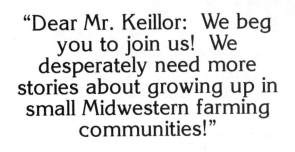

"Dear Mr. Keillor: We beg
you to join us! We
desperately need more
stories about growing up in
small Midwestern farming
communities!"

Hesston College engineering students are continuing their work on a horse-drawn submarine.

Theological Softball

Many churches sponsor softball teams to play in a church league. The purpose of these leagues is to encourage informal fellowship, comradery, and teamwork. For Mennonites, softball is an acceptable catharsis for aggression. You can work out your hostilities under the banner of sportsmanship. Other denominations, which are not usually pacifist, are no match for competitive Mennonites.

What if each denomination approached the game of softball with its own theological emphasis?

> Calvinists believe the game is fixed.
> Lutherans believe they can't win, but trust the
>   Scorekeeper.
> Quakers won't swing.
> Shiites strike out.
> Pentecostals pop up and fly out.

Presbyterians go over most people's heads.
Unitarians can catch anything.
Amish walk a lot.
Pagans sacrifice.
Jehovah's Witnesses are thrown out often.
Grace Brethren think they're always safe.
Christian Scientists are off base.
Televangelists get caught stealing.
Methodists try to reach second.
Episcopalians pass the plate.
Evangelicals make effective pitches.
Fundamentalists balk.
Mormons are in left field.
Dunkers are down by 3.
Adventists have a 7th inning stretch.
Hutterites have the best teamwork.
Old Order Mennonite ministers sit on the bench.
Atheists refuse to have an Umpire.
Baptists want to play hardball.
Premillennialists expect the game to be called soon
        on account of darkness.
The pope claims never to commit an error.
In the batting order, Mennonites should follow Christ.

Where's Menno?
at the Relief Sale

MennoSights

$.95,U.S./$.99,Canada/65p,U.K.   October 29, 1993

Was it really Menno who addressed a gathering of scholars via satellite last spring?

Modern-Day Menno Sightings Continue!!

  Much attention has been given to the fate of Menno Simons during the past decade (see August 21, 1983 *National Inquirer,* p. 4.). Although interest in the subject has waned during the past 24 months, the question still hangs on the lips of many: Is Menno really dead?

  "Actually, that is a very valid and open question," said Eli Burkholder, Director of

continued on page 2

1

the Institute of Mennonite Subtleties, Elkhart, Indiana, in a recent phone conversation. "In fact, Menno sightings have not dropped off in the past two years at all."

The Institute, which gathers and tabulates information on reported sightings of Menno Simons across North America, has received word of 19 appearances of the reformer since January 1, 1992.

Mennonite Central Committee (MCC) in Akron, Pennsylvania, collects information on international Simons' sightings. Menno is usually spotted doing relief work in Third World nations, but occasionally turns up in his native Friesland. One spurious claim from Perth, Australia, later proved to be a vacationing and aging Tim Conway.

Most North American sightings seem to follow a pattern, Burkholder said. Being a true Mennonite, Simons is most often seen at stores which are either having a sale or giving something away free. Six sightings have involved strawberry pie purchases at one of seven different MCC relief sales.

The most recent sighting of Menno was at a Saskatoon, Saskatchewan, service station Kwik-Mart where he allegedly bought all five ingredients necessary to prepare every recipe in the *More-with-Less Cookbook*.

What makes people think that they have actually seen Menno?

"Often they aren't really sure," says Joe

continued on page 3

2

Springer, historian and curator at the Mennonite Historical Library, Goshen, Indiana. "I've spent considerable time looking over a lot of the reports myself and it seems that there is often some confusion—was it really Menno, or Elvis with a beard? Many people who claim to have seen him [Simons] also believe they've seen the King."

Menno was seen at The People's Place in the summer of 1991 by veteran staff member Norma Gehman. "There was just this guy sitting in the lobby doing nothing. I assumed it was another one of the summer's confused tourists. Only later did I realize, 'Hey, that was the former Witmarsum priest!'"

"A familiar story," Burkholder said upon hearing Gehman's account. "Most people realize it later. They're just casually looking through a Mennonite history text or examining some old woodcuts or engravings they have lying around the house, and they realize they've seen him earlier that morning."

"A good historical tip-off for Menno-watching is his walking with a crutch," added Springer. "This is pretty clear from the documentation. Also, he charges only on Diner's Club, never American Express. I haven't been able to trace that practice to any of his pre-Wismar writings, however."

Any number of theories exist as to why

continued on page 4

3

Menno, if alive, hasn't gone public. Some say he's waiting for an MC-GC merger. Others think he's just hanging around for the right potluck invitation. A third theory holds that the nearly 500-year-old is waiting for an apartment to open at Glencroft Retirement Community, Glendale, Arizona.

If Simons should go public, Mennonite Mutual Aid's vice president for advertising, Esther Toews, hopes to snag the radical reformer for an endorsement campaign.

"We could really do some great things with him on film," Toews said. "I've prepared a tentative script. We're ready to shoot as soon as he's ready to come in from the cold." Mennonite Economic Development Associates, Menno Travel Service, and Penn Alps, Inc. have all expressed interest in having Simons appear in their own advertising and promotional campaigns. It has also been rumored that Menno may even be the subject of a forthcoming Oliver Stone film.

Will Simons "come in from the cold?"

"I doubt it," says Burkholder. "At this point, my personal feeling is that he's living in an above-garage apartment in Buffalo, New York, with Bruce Lee, Elvis, Buddy Holly, and Jim Morrison."

4

What's the Difference Between the Amish and the Mennonites?

New Mennonites sometimes find that their families and friends think they've joined the Amish. In fact, Mennonites themselves aren't always sure *how* the two groups differ. The comparative list below offers a glimpse of some of the subtler distinctions.

Amish	Mennonites
☞ live in the country and visit the city.	☞ live in the suburbs and visit the country.
☞ sing Anabaptist hymns.	☞ sing Protestant hymns.
☞ are easily identified by their uniform black pants and solid-colored shirts.	☞ are easily identified by their uniform blue jeans and flannel shirts.
☞ have last names like Yoder, Miller, and Beiler.	☞ have last names like Yoder, Miller, and Byler.
☞ draw worldwide attention by their simple way of life.	☞ don't.
☞ foul the air with tobacco smoke.	☞ foul the air with exhaust fumes.
☞ mostly were raised in Amish families.	☞ often were raised in Amish families.
☞ read the *Martyrs Mirror*.	☞ have heard of the *Martyrs Mirror*.
☞ attract interest from outsiders.	☞ earn interest from outsiders.
☞ are wild and rowdy as youths, but later join the church.	☞ "get saved" as youths, and later leave the church.
☞ use more animal fertilizer.	☞ are more careful to refer to it as "manure."

Honey, I Shrunk the Amish!

Identifying an Identifiable Identity

The following article on the topic of Mennonite Identity was originally slated for publication in *The Mennonite Encyclopedia*, vol. 5 (Herald Press, 1990), but was inadvertently omitted. So the guys at Scottdale called us up and asked if we could get it into print for them. We eagerly agreed since the subject of Mennonite Identity is one with which every New Mennonite must quickly become acquainted. It's not that New Mennonites care that much about "Identity." However, they will soon discover that discussing Mennonite Identity is the overriding, if not obsessive, preoccupation of most other Mennonites. This article is typical of the current dialogue. (For those who own the *Mennonite Encyclopedia*, vol. 5, please insert this article at page 413.)

Identity, Mennonite. Perhaps no other topic has elicited more conversation, dialogue, input, discussion, reflection, journaling, sharing, internal processing, or PC printer paper output than has the subject of Mennonite identity. Are Mennonites losing touch with themselves? Were they ever in touch with themselves? When? If so, was that a bad thing? Why? These and many other perplexing complexities have driven some contemporary Mennonites to the brink of the Anabaptist abyss and thrust identity to the forefront of every Mennonite agenda. This article will outline some of the major questions which have marked the intense interest in Mennonite identity during the years since the publication of *The Mennonite Encyclopedia,* volumes I-IV (1955-59). Attention will also be given to major writers and publications in the field, and an assessment of their various impacts on all phases of the life of the church with regard to identity. Conditionally, this essay will briefly summarize Mennonite identity as it is now understood most widely in the church at large.

Identity is the major question facing the larger Mennonite church as it enters the twenty-first century. A veritable explosion of interest in identity marked the 1980s and '90s. But while identity was the subject of nearly 3,675 articles and 59 books from the Mennonite pen and press between 1985 and 1990 alone, it did not suddenly rise to such prominence without a long and laborious background of interest and investigation. Since the days of the earliest Anabaptists, Mennonites have regularly asked (quite frankly), "Who am I?" For example, speculation has circulated for several decades among both European and North American Anabaptist scholars regarding Obbe Philips' sudden disappearance from the North German circle of re-baptizers. Much of the scholarly weight now suggests that questions of identity played a larger-than-previously-thought part in Obbe's defection. Identity was also the subject of a recently discovered treatise by Menno himself, written in the last years of his life and running some 111 pages in the reformer's tightly scrawled hand. Menno was as concerned about identity as are his spiritual children, it now seems.

Questions of identity followed Mennonites for generations. Might internal rumblings and stirrings of a latent identity have led Mennonites to North America in 1683 and 1874? "The links are definitely there," wrote Ralph Z. Zook in the introduction to his recent (1990) dissertation, "Identity, Ideation, Idealogues, and Idaho: Themes in Mennonite Migratory Patterns and Practices."

Yet, despite its presence in Mennonite literature, visual arts, biblical exegesis, and subconscious group personality, identity has taken on a new prominence in Mennonite life in recent decades. In his ground-breaking 1950 article, "Mennonites: Identifying and Identifiable Identity," Paul J. Kauffman suggested that Mennonite identity would be the single most important topic among Mennonites in the post-war era. Though never styling himself as a self-styled prophet, Kauffman spoke with prophetic clarity what a generation of Mennonites have echoed in the years since his landmark treatise. Rarely has a Mennonite writer put his or her proverbial finger more squarely on the point of tension in which so many Mennonites found themselves after 1945.

With the war over and a new sense of national identity thrust upon them, Mennonites in the post-war period groped about for a new identity as followers of Menno Simons. The old identity markers of the previous century and a half, while serving to clearly mark identity in terms unambiguous for those times, seemed ill-fitted for the more complex and rigorous task of identity during the 1950s, 1960s, 1970s, 1980s, and 1990s. In fact, those previously useful identity markers seemed generally useless for the balance of the twentieth century.

Obviously, the years which have followed 1950 have been ones filled with numerous identity quests and questions. The rise in Mennonite interest in identity roughly paralleled the rise in general socioeconomic status, urbanization, and social, political, and psychological acculturation among Mennonites of the same period. Detailed studies of these and other connecting and corroborating motifs and images in Mennonite identity have proven beyond doubt that the intense interest in questions of Mennonite identity during this period are linked to other aspects of influences—both internal and external—on Mennonite peoplehood in the last half of the twentieth century.

In conclusion, Mennonites today view their own sense of identity as an important indicator of their church's health and vitality. That a clear sense of community, peoplehood, and empowered congregational visioning grow out of a well-defined, clearly understood, and widely discussed positive identity, most Mennonites now accept as axiomatic. Giving leadership to identity matters in the local fellowship is generally seen as a priority item. Among most Mennonites currently groping about for a new identity amid the collapse of larger-community-identification, searching for one's relationship to other persons and institutions has become not only a spiritual pilgrimage, but also, in many cases, an identity in itself.

Much of the attention to the subject of Mennonite identity has come from increased notice among Mennonite constituent groups that less of what constitutes and defines the core Mennonite image remains conditionally intact. In the rapidly changing and mobile world in which western society finds itself as only one part, individual and group identity becomes all the more critical. The need for a clearer Mennonite identity was outlined in Esther K. Tschetter's 1977 thesis, "Identity, Ideology, Ideograms, and Idumea in Mennonite Perspective." Tschetter identified identity as foundational to any coherent and cognitive sense of self which may be gained and maintained through committed peoplehood. Contrasting false and true identity, Tschetter set the tone of future Mennonite identity studies, by suggesting that true identity (rather than false) was the worthwhile focus of any future identity investigation.

Following in Tschetter's footsteps, several Mennonite institutions mounted massive campaigns to identify and illuminate what they saw as a true Mennonite identity worthy of community implementation and discussion. The inter-Mennonite Institute of Mennonite Subtleties sponsored a 1989 speakers' forum on the subject, "Identity: Can We Afford Not to Care?" The well-received series looked at various ways in which Mennonite identity has been at play in our collective past. Identifying subthemes in Mennonite self-understanding, speakers suggested connections between loss of identity and changing ideology. Identity can be lost, the speakers said, but it can also be found again.

In the hope of finding a new Mennonite identity in the very process of creating one, a subcommittee of the Inter-Mennonite Consortium and Coordinating Committee for Identity and Indemnity established a standing Identity Council (IC of the IMCCCII). Knowing that identity is key to any sense of self-understanding, the group focused on identifying what it was that had held Mennonites together. Ideally, they noted that identity rises from within a group, although most people groups also receive some impulses (however enigmatic) from surrounding socio-political influences. Identity will continue to be one of the chief issues facing the church, the Council concluded in its 450-page report.

The connection between personal and group identity has been the focus of recent studies in Mennonite identity. Much of this work was summarized in by John Freud Funk. The connection between the internal and external is clear enough to most Mennonites, although few are accustomed to thinking in terms of external identity developing in concert with that of the internal. Further study is needed in the field of Mennonite psychological exigencies and identity as it relates to internal and external developmental theory, yet the foundation has been provided and no time should be lost in the fulfillment of this critical area of identity research, critical as it is to the development of wholesome and wholistic identity among Mennonites.

Viewed from a post-constructionist perspective, Mennonite identity serves as a guiding principle in the absence of a consensus theory of church polity. While based on a community ideal, theoretically, the Mennonite identity as seen by the majority only enhances and redefines the impact of what others already noticed was core material. One could, of course, ask (as many have), why is identity so critical to Mennonite peoplehood at this juncture of our pilgrimage as a people? More than likely, the answers to that question would be as multifaceted as the multi-sided query itself. Certainly any attempt to answer such a question could only lead to further analysis of the central problem of Mennonitism itself. At this point in time, the question of Mennonite identity remains important for its own sake, whether or not further related questions are pursued.

In summarizing Mennonite identity as understood by many Mennonites at present, one must begin by acknowledging that identity has a variety of foci, all of which are relevant to the Mennonite experience. Yet the ability and necessity of some aspects to match our current situation requires a serious attempt at summarization. Among Mennonites grappling with the issue, identifying identity in terms useful for its subsequent analysis has been the most critical component of investigation. Identity, whether lost or in process, has been a most significant item in any Mennonite agenda. Mennonites are held together by a common identity which defies identification. Without the ability to fully grasp or enumerate its parts, Mennonites are cognitively aware that an identity of great consequence binds them together. The unseen, though much studied, identity of the church will continue to elucidate and illuminate Mennonite thinking on the subject, while eluding any firm attempt to precisely define its identifiable features.

A new Mennonite group,
the Slam-Dunkers,
is growing rapidly in Indiana.

Johann introduces
CORNIES

NEW!

From the first name in Russian Mennonite Agriculture

Johann CORNIES
BREAKFAST CEREAL

A NUTRITION TRADITION FROM THE STEPPES TO THE PLAINS

SEND 2 BOXTOPS!

To: Fast Foods Co.
1860 West Way
Corn, Oklahoma

(This is not an offer. We're just trying to save a few boxtops.)

FREE INSIDE! Martyr Action Figures! (NON-FLAMMABLE)

NET WT. 262g

Try our new
TURKEY RED WHEAT CRISPS
They're like Zwieback in a bowl!

Top Ten Amish Quilt Patterns and/or Beatles Hits

10. Octopus' Garden
9. Sunshine and Shadow
8. Drunkard's Path
7. Lucy in the Sky with Diamonds
6. The Long and Winding Road
5. Double Wedding Ring
4. Strawberry Fields Forever
3. Old Brown Shoe
2. Carolina Lily
1. (tie) Helter Skelter / Crazy

Peoplehood and Heritage Quiz

1. Many Mennonites spend a lifetime
   a) in service to others.
   b) working for the church.
   c) getting over the fact that they're Mennonite.

2. Few Mennonites have ever read
   a) *Playboy*.
   b) *The National Enquirer*.
   c) Anabaptist writings.

3. Mennonites are most often confused by the many
   a) small splinter groups among us.
   b) inter-Mennonite periodicals.
   c) ways to spell Klassen/Klaassen/Classen/
      Claassen/Clasen/etc.

4. Mennonites in the U.S. think that Winnipeg is
   a) the capital of Manitoba.
   b) a Mecca for Mennonites.
   c) a contest for pirates.

5. Tourists to Amish country will most likely return
   home with
   a) pleasant memories of the simple life.
   b) a lovely Amish quilt.
   c) something on their sneakers.

6. Five centuries of Mennonite suffering, steadfastness,
   and wandering have given the world
   a) the separation of church and state.
   b) a testimony of nonviolence.
   c) great recipes.

7. New Mennonites are often disappointed to discover that
    a) some Old Order groups condone cigar smoking.
    b) some "liberal" groups condone Bermuda shorts.
    c) no group condones *both* cigar smoking *and* Bermuda shorts.

8. The phrase "the upside-down kingdom" pertains to
    a) the teachings of Jesus.
    b) a book by Donald Kraybill.
    c) the flying of the Canadian flag at the '92 World Series.

9. Throughout their history the Hutterites have struggled to find
    a) ways to share their property.
    b) places to live in peace.
    c) clothing to match polka dots.

10. Some Mennonites believe "the Community of Goods" refers to
    a) Christian mutual aid.
    b) a Hutterite practice.
    c) The People's Place.

2.
Lifestyle

Mennonites have long been known as a "peculiar people," a distinct ethno-religious group, a sect. While many Mennonites have labored tirelessly to discard any vestige of the ancestors' "nonconformity" to the world, being different seems to die hard. Today, aspects of Mennonite "lifestyle" set Mennonites apart as much as did their forebears' attention to physical nonconformity. While a Mennonite lifestyle may seem subtle and relatively unimportant, it serves as an effective boundary marker. You're sure to feel like an outsider until you master the Mennonite lifestyle habits.

In this section you will learn . . .

. . . about acceptable Mennonite recreation and tips for taking cheap vacations.

. . . the importance of saving and collecting everything.

. . . how to state any objective reality in terms of a personal subjective experience.

. . . how to effectively "affirm," "reflect," "share," "touch base," and "facilitate" within the "broader faith community."

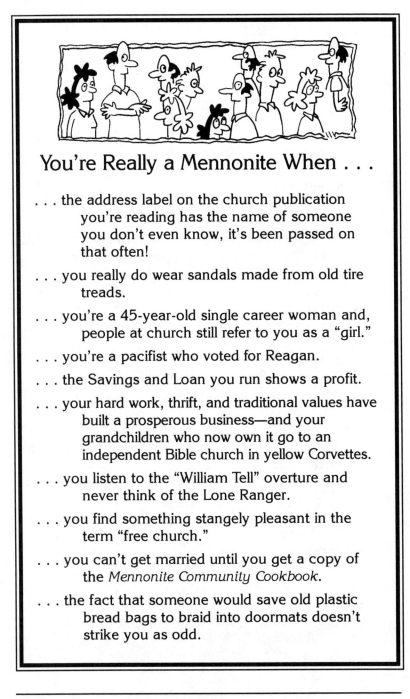

You're Really a Mennonite When . . .

. . . the address label on the church publication you're reading has the name of someone you don't even know, it's been passed on that often!

. . . you really do wear sandals made from old tire treads.

. . . you're a 45-year-old single career woman and, people at church still refer to you as a "girl."

. . . you're a pacifist who voted for Reagan.

. . . the Savings and Loan you run shows a profit.

. . . your hard work, thrift, and traditional values have built a prosperous business—and your grandchildren who now own it go to an independent Bible church in yellow Corvettes.

. . . you listen to the "William Tell" overture and never think of the Lone Ranger.

. . . you find something stangely pleasant in the term "free church."

. . . you can't get married until you get a copy of the *Mennonite Community Cookbook*.

. . . the fact that someone would save old plastic bread bags to braid into doormats doesn't strike you as odd.

Acceptable and Unacceptable
Mennonite Vacations

1. **Acceptable:**
   Taking the family to the Grand Canyon.
   Unacceptable:
   Slipping off to Vegas.

2. **Unacceptable:**
   An expensive pleasure trip to Disney World.
   Acceptable:
   An expensive pleasure trip to Disney World which includes stopping to visit your grandmother in Sarasota, Florida.

3. **Acceptable:**
   Traveling coast-to-coast with the *Mennonite Your Way Directory.*
   Unacceptable:
   Shiftlessly drifting around the country with the *Mennonite Your Way Directory.*

4. **Acceptable:**
   Camping on the weekend with your small group.
   Unacceptable:
   Camping on the weekend with your reserve unit.

5. **Unacceptable:**
   An extravagant cruise in the Mediterranean.
   Acceptable:
   A tour of the Holy Land.

6. **Acceptable:**
   Attending any church conference assembly.
   Unacceptable:
   Attending a Star Trek convention.

7. **Acceptable:**
   Taking a week off work to raise homes in a disaster area.
   Unacceptable:
   Taking a week off work to raise cain and create a disaster area.

8. **Acceptable:**
   Following a Mennonite tour group in Europe.
   Unacceptable:
   Following a rock group on its European tour (except U2, which is marginally acceptable).

9. **Unacceptable:**
   An African safari.
   Acceptable:
   A short-term Voluntary Service assignment at a mission station in Africa.

10. **Marginally acceptable:**
    A tour of a winery.
    Unacceptable:
    A tour of a brewery.

11. **Unacceptable:**
    Gambling in a casino in Atlantic City.
    Newly Acceptable:
    Competing in the Miss America Pageant in Atlantic City.

Top Ten Things Mennonites Save and Re-use Way Too Often

10. Aluminum foil
9. Plastic tablewear
8. File folders
7. Yogurt containers
6. Brown mailing envelopes
5. Bread bag twist-ties
4. Plastic drinking straws
3. Gift wrapping paper
2. Styrofoam meat trays
1. Tea bags

The MCC Re-uzit Pottery Shop.

Many Are Called . . . But Few Are Chosen

Mennobabble

Much has been studied and written regarding the change from Low German and Pennsylvania Dutch to English, as new generations of Mennonites have come along. But the change from English to Mennobabble has been taking place in some quarters almost without notice. Like the old German dialects, this new dialect of Psychobabble helps to establish community boundaries, allowing everyone to know who the insiders are and, of course, who is an outsider. (New Mennonites will need to learn quickly!)

Mennobabble is also the official language of the Borrowed Trendy Spirituality Club, because it is naturally suited to express any fact of the objective world in terms of one's inner self.

If there is a drawback to Mennobabble, it would be its limited vocabulary, forcing the speaker to fall back on the same words over and over again.

You may soon encounter a conversation in Mennobabble, much like the one recorded below.

Luke: Richard and Sarah! Hi! Do you enjoy this place often?

Richard: Yes, we come here to experience the seafood almost every week.

Luke: Well, you're just the persons I was feeling the need to get with sometime soon.

Sarah: Do you have a concern to share?

Luke: I was hoping we might touch base to set up a time to sit with our small group and process some of the issues that are being dealt with and worked through in the wider faith community.

Sarah: I want to affirm your concern and say that I believe

A Mennonite engages in
serious reflection.

we can feel a real spirit of community around this if we'll just let ourselves.

Richard: Let me affirm you both and add that I have faith that as we walk together we can really facilitate each other in this process.

Luke: Am I hearing you say that we need to be more intentional in our shepherding?

Richard: Yes, and let me just say in addition that we need to reflect more upon the giftedness of each individual to discern where each is at in each one's own spiritual pilgrimage, especially in relation to lifestyle issues.

Luke: I hear what you're saying, and I'd just like to respond to that by saying that we need to connect more with persons where they're at, to resource them for their ministries in the body. I can share with you that I've been journaling about this issue for some time.

Sarah: I think I'm hearing both of you say we need to be careful not to forget the special needs of individuals, while we're visioning for the whole community. I would affirm you in that. Maybe you could give more leadership to that.

Luke: But let me also say that we need to integrate these gifts and persons into ministry by enabling and facilitating one another in meaningful, inclusive relationships.

Sarah: Well, I sense a real spirit of connecting here. Let's keep reflecting and dialoguing on these issues. After all, I think we want everyone to have a sense of ownership in ministry—

Richard: If whether it's pastoring, nurturing, peace-and-justice making, or just *being*.

Luke: I affirm you on that. Well, I'm feeling the need to go.

Richard: Second door on the left.

Luke: No, I mean I must leave. I have a meeting I need to be at.

Richard: Oh, I hear what you're saying. Well, let's touch base again soon.

Luke: I hope your seafood turns out to be a good experience for you!

Sarah: Thanks!

Mennonite Out-Of-Your-Way Directory

Travel has been an integral part of the Mennonite experience for over 450 years. Of course the early Anabaptists traveled mostly at night, or as a result of state banishment orders, but today's Mennonites who spend summers in Europe, the Holy Land, or the Caribbean feel as though they're keeping up a centuries-old religious tradition.

The Benefits

For the cost-conscious Mennonite, staying with fellow church members (instead of motels) serves as an economical way to see the country. Stopping to visit with other Mennonites gives one the possibility of scavenging other money-saving tips on fuel, food, and sightseeing. Who better to direct you to the lowest prices in town than a local Mennonite resident?

It is important to take care to pronounce your host's town's name correctly. As peaceful as Mennonites generally are, many can become quite agitated and even violent upon hearing their community's name mispronounced. Do yourself a favor and practice saying your destination's name at least 120 times before even making plans to drive there. You'll be glad you did.

The Fun

For added fun: As you travel, ask your hosts if they have relatives in the next town you're stopping in. See if you can crisscross North America, using only one extended family as your hosts! A Mennonite-Out-of-Your-Way Tour can be taken virtually anywhere there are other Mennonites; the tour outlined below is only a sample.

Begin in Washington, D.C. (pronounced: "WASH-ing-ton," not "WORSH-ing-ton"). Visit well-known Mennonite sights in the U.S. capital, such as the Washington Community Fellowship Church, the Mennonite Central Committee Washington Center, and the Office of Senator Mark Hatfield.

David Letterman examines
a copy of the new
*Mennonite Out-Of-Your-Way
Directory.*

The Relatives

Heading north into Pennsylvania, stop by Lancaster (pronounced: "LANK-uh-stir") and Ephrata (pronounced: "F-ruh-tuh"). A favorite and exciting pastime with your hosts here will be trying to discover how you and they are related. Warning: It may really confuse your Lancaster-area Mennonite hosts if it turns out that you are not related to them. Most Lancaster Mennonites believe that all Mennonites originally came from Lancaster and may challenge your claim of church membership, should your surname not appear somewhere on their family tree.

Elsewhere in Pennsylvania, take time to stop in the Kishacoquillas Valley (pronounced: "Big Valley"). Become acquainted with the wide variety of Mennonite and Amish groups clustered here. Each fellowship is distinct and unique. Yet even here, amid division and diversity, all Anabaptist churches—no matter what their surface differences—are still united by the timeless Mennonite Creed: "If it costs something, I don't want it; if it's free, I'll take two." (Incidentally, this classic statement of Mennonite core values still serves as the basis for all inter-Mennonite cooperative efforts and denominational integration moves.)

Venture next into Ontario and stay in the Waterloo (pronounced: "Water-LOO," not "WATER-loo") Mennonite community. Stop in at Conrad Grebel College, founded 1961. Do note that CGC is the only institution of higher learning in the world which is named after a college drop-out who spent his unproductive university days brawling and partying.

The Gifts

Westward and into Ohio, drop by Berlin (pronounced: "BER-lin," not "Ber-LIN") in Holmes County.

While traveling, do remember to bring a host gift for each family you impose upon. This might require an initial investment during your first several trips; however, after you yourself have served as an out-of-your-way host, you will receive things which you will gladly want to pass along to others. Recycling host family gifts in this way saves time, money, and wrapping paper.

In Nebraska, be sure to stop in Beatrice (pronounced: "be-AT-ris"). Enjoy your visit among the corn huskers, but don't bother looking for the Nebraska Amish here. You missed them back in the Kishacoquillas Valley.

The Debate

While you're in the Great Plains, a Mennonite community you might want to visit in Kansas is Moundridge. During the nineteenth century, Mennonites argued vigorously over whether the area seemed more like a mound or a ridge. The town's name was coined by a Mennonite Conciliation Service team sent in to settle things down and come up with a compromise. While you're in the area, why not make your own assessment and join in the debate! Send your choice to: The Mound-Ridge Debate, c/o Mennonite Conciliation Services, Unity, ON, A2Z 1N2.

The Epitome

As you continue to explore the wider North American Mennonite world, why not visit a congregation which claims to be the epitome of Mennonitism? Journey to the Superb Mennonite Church in Kerrobert, Saskatchewan. Experience worship with this superb group of Mennonites. Find out why they have been able to maintain such a superb church life together. Sing superb hymns, hear a superb sermon, and give to a superb church treasury. Perhaps you'll even be invited to stay for a superb dinner afterwards.

Two provinces to the west lies British Columbia, home to several dozen Mennonite Brethren and Conference of Mennonites in Canada congregations. The Frazer River Valley is home to most Mennonites in this part of Canada. A note to the New Mennonite: ALWAYS refer to British Columbia as "B.C." Using the province's full name will instantly mark you as an outsider in Canadian Mennonite circles.

End your trip with a visit to Nome (pronounced: "Gnome"), Alaska. There really isn't any Mennonite connection to Nome, but this is about as out-of-your-way as the tour gets.

Sue —
Please give this book to Lester N. at church.

Lester —
Take to Sarah at work on Monday.

Sarah —
when Martin K. comes in, have him drop it off when he goes past Mary's.

Mary —
Happy Reading !!!
Please return book when you are finished. Love, Carol
P.S. Great book !!!

The Mennonite Postal System

Lifestyle Quiz

1. Mennonite readers acquired this book by
   a) purchasing it at the Faith and Life Bookstore.
   b) ordering it from Good Books.
   c) borrowing it from someone who borrowed it from his sister whose roommate got it from her church library.

2. The television show which best resonated with Mennonite values was
   a) The Waltons.
   b) Little House on the Prairie.
   c) Let's Make a Deal.

3. If Sarah Landis marries Tom Yoder, she will be known to Mennonites as
   a) Mrs. Tom Yoder.
   b) Sarah Landis-Yoder.
   c) both of the above, depending on who's talking.

4. Mennonite artists spend long hours working in
   a) private studios.
   b) college art departments.
   c) restaurants.

5. In Mennonite circles, when "A" phones "B" with a message for "B" to call "C," it means that
   a) there is important news at church.
   b) a group decision is being made.
   c) "A" doesn't want to make a pay call.

6. Mennonite employers hire people who
   a) are hardworking and conscientious.
   b) are experienced and educated.
   c) work cheap and don't smoke.

7. Mennonites inspired by MCC are likely to have
    a) an international perspective.
    b) a passion for justice.
    c) all the SELF HELP Crafts jewelry their bodies can
       support.

8. A Mennonite who has a full-time job, a half-time
       job, and responsibilities at church is
    a) a responsible, ambitious worker.
    b) a workaholic.
    c) a pastor.

9. A Mennonite who spends two consecutive evenings
       at home
    a) is a family-oriented person.
    b) is recovering from an illness.
    c) has had a meeting cancelled.

10. Mennonites seldom laugh at
    a) dirty jokes.
    b) themselves.
    c) material in this book.

3.
Religious Activities

Mennonites are a devoutly religious people. Practices such as believers baptism have distinguished Mennonites from Protestants and Catholics for centuries. Other religious traditions have been added and integrated into the Mennonite religious experience more recently. As a New Mennonite you will need to familiarize yourself with today's religious activities. You'll also want to learn about which religious traditions have fallen out of vogue among Mennonites and which ones never were all that cherished.

In this section you will learn . . .

. . . which religious traditions Mennonites are glad *not* to have.

. . . how much you know about Mennonite missionaries.

. . . how to unload your old church meetinghouse.

. . . how politically conservative and liberal Mennonites view themselves.

You're Really a Mennonite When . . .

. . . you carry a Bible and a mug to Sunday school.

. . . your small group meeting has been cancelled and the first evening you're all clear to meet again is in six weeks.

. . . you're a regular at Campus Crusade meetings, yet consider yourself an Anabaptist.

. . . your pastor is listed by your district conference as a deaconess.

. . . you realize that Salunga is not a dessert.

. . . you think that Lent is a good time of the year to borrow money from Catholics.

Liturgical Kick-boxing

Mennonite Missionaries' Quiz

1. **A missionary couple's greatest challenge is to**
   a) learn a new language.
   b) overcome culture shock.
   c) stay married after packing the suitcase.

2. **Many missionaries sent by Mennonite church agencies are** *not*
   a) ordained ministers.
   b) medical doctors.
   c) Mennonites.

3. **Relief workers differ from missionaries in that**
   a) they are sent by different agencies.
   b) relief workers serve fewer terms.
   c) missionaries wear shoes.

4. **Missionaries in remote places are "happy" to receive**
   a) back issues of magazines.
   b) visitors from the mission board.
   c) used tea bags.

5. **Missionaries get frustrated dealing with**
   a) new political situations.
   b) new foods.
   c) new missionaries.

6. **New missionaries can be easily identified when they**
   a) make cultural blunders.
   b) have trouble translating.
   c) still remove bugs from their soup.

7. Missionaries find it hardest to share
    a) the gospel cross-culturally.
    b) adminstrative duties with local Christians.
    c) the Land Rover with other missionaries.

8. Returned missionaries' evening slide programs are often accompanied by the sound of
    a) natives singing in simple huts.
    b) exotic wildlife in game preserves.
    c) cars starting in the church parking lot.

Religious Traditions Mennonites Would *Like* To Have

- Christmas Eve midnight mass
- meditation
- passing the peace
- love feast
- Lent
- ordination of women

Religious Traditions Mennonites Wish They Did *Not* Have

- footwashing
- Sunday school
- the holy kiss
- revival meetings
- plain clothing
- ordination of women

Religious Traditions Mennonites are *Glad* Not To Have

- infant baptism
- ceremonial circumcision
- celibacy
- animal sacrifice
- vegetarianism
- the jihad
- snake handling
- the peyote ceremony
- ordination of women

OUR CHURCH CAN BE YOUR CHURCH!

Is your new independent fellowship looking for a church building?

Due to increased Mennonite demand for upscale Protestant-style sanctuaries, we now have hundreds of functional, low-priced historic meeting houses available!

With a few simple touches you can make any of them look like a *real* church. Just add a steeple, and you too can have a true "temple made with hands!"

Contact:
MENNONITE BORED OF
CONGREGATIONAL
MINISTRIES
(515)FOR-SALE

Passing on our heritage
for a quarter
of a century.

A Parable Paraphrased

"Two Mennonites went up front in church to pray; the one a conservative and the other a liberal. The conservative stood and prayed thus with himself:

'God, I thank Thee that I am not as other Mennonites are—humanistic, unscriptural, immoral—or even as this liberal. I watch Christian broadcasting twice a week, I give them tithes of all that I possess, which is much since Thou hast prospered me as a reward for clean living. I protest abortion and have adopted unwanted babies. I support missionaries overseas and attend revivals at home. . .'

* * *

And the liberal stood and prayed thus with himself:

'God, I thank you that I am not as other Mennonites are—militaristic, materialistic, sexist—or even as this Republican. I fast for El Salvador twice a week, I give to MCC tithes of all that I possess, which isn't much since I'm trying to identify with the poor and avoid paying war taxes. I protest the death penalty and visit those in prison. I support SELF HELP craftspeople overseas and attend strategy meetings for all the correct causes at home . . . '

* * *

Which of these went home justified?"

Your family can be our family.

We Mennonites like to think of ourselves as a diverse and growing church. That's really not the case, however, and that's where you come in.

We're looking for families—big families—who are interested in joining a Mennonite church. It doesn't matter whether you're white, black, brown, red, or yellow. We have an image to create, and you can be an important part of it!

Bring your family into our family; you'll be proud—and so will we.

YOUR FACE HERE

MENNONITES BORED of MISSIONS
500 S. Suburban Way
Elk's Heart, IN 46517

If you don't have a family, that's okay too . . . a Mennonite church is a great place to meet your potential mate!

Religious Activities Quiz

1. Mennonites who drive to church slowly, are trying to avoid
   a) thinking frantic thoughts before worship.
   b) receiving a speeding ticket.
   c) spilling the crock pot over the upholstery.

2. When everyone arrives on time for Sunday school, it indicates that
   a) the class has a talented teacher.
   b) class members are eager to get together.
   c) people forgot to change their clocks back to Standard Time.

3. At the front of the church, Mennonite worshipers will likely see
   a) a wooden cross.
   b) an open Bible.
   c) some sickly ferns.

4. Congregations adjust their pastors' incomes based on
   a) the cost of living index.
   b) the number of dependents.
   c) "Living More With Less."

5. The Mennonite ordinance using the most water is
   a) baptism.
   b) footwashing.
   c) the holy kiss.

6. When choosing Sunday school curricula, Mennonites are most concerned with
   a) the materials' doctrinal content.
   b) the writer's theological assumptions.
   c) whether or not it has color pictures.

7. A junior high Sunday school teacher will make a
   dozen phone calls to
   a) inform the class of a special event.
   b) locate a suitable teaching resource.
   c) find a willing substitute teacher.

8. "Four-part harmony" refers to
   a) a style of singing.
   b) the consensus of the Gospels.
   c) how ushers collect the offering.

9. At church, when the women get up while the men
   stay seated, it's time to
   a) hear from the women's choir.
   b) separate for footwashing.
   c) clean up after the fellowship meal.

10. A person unable to leave a Mennonite worship
    service probably
    a) has been deeply moved by the sermon and music.
    b) is having a mystical experience.
    c) got a thumb stuck in the communion cup rack.

4.
Institutions

From their Radical Reformation roots Mennonites have long been suspicious of church institutions and bureaucracy. But finally after four hundred years, Mennonites were able to overcome their misgivings and resolutely set out to build an institutional world of the highest order. Today church institutions play an even greater role as they now effectively provide the very glue which holds Mennonites together. Make no mistake, Mennonite institutions are the forces and fortresses with which every New Mennonite (NM) will quickly need to become quite familiar.

In this section you will learn . . .

. . . who's who among the Mennonites and why.

. . . how to select the Mennonite periodicals which will most handily confirm your prejudices.

. . . about AIMM's EMC, EMCC, EMMC, GC, MBM/S and FEBC connections.

. . . which prominent Mennonites are related to the most other prominent Mennonites.

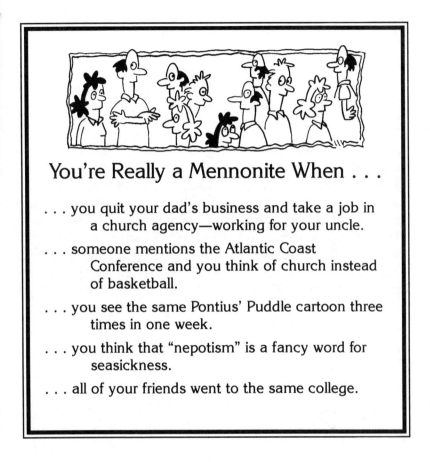

You're Really a Mennonite When . . .

. . . you quit your dad's business and take a job in a church agency—working for your uncle.

. . . someone mentions the Atlantic Coast Conference and you think of church instead of basketball.

. . . you see the same Pontius' Puddle cartoon three times in one week.

. . . you think that "nepotism" is a fancy word for seasickness.

. . . all of your friends went to the same college.

Macronyms

One of the first tasks facing any New Mennonite (NM) is that of becoming familiar with Mennonite acronyms (MACRONYMS). Mennonites use MACRONYMS for the sake of simplicity, frugality, and ecology (less ink and paper wasted, etc.). Despite their clear practical and theological Anabaptist rootings, MACRONYMS have occasionally caused some confusion for the uninitiated. Generally, however, the meaning of a MACRONYM is explicitly clear in context, as any NM can see in the following typical news release in a Mennonite magazine.

MCC, et al., OK Co-op at AMBS

CEOS May Act
to KO Snafus

On May 11, 1993, MBM and COM convened an open meeting of MCC constituent groups. Gathered on the campus of AMBS, the 200 delegates arrived from as far away as PEI and LA in RVs. Reporters from *MWR, GH, MBH, MHB,* and *FQ* were on hand for p.r. as well.

Citing a recent MQR article in her opening address, the meeting's m.c. (an MB from BC) asked how Mennonites might cooperate more effectively. She then called on EMMC and GC [ed. note: GCMC, not MBE's GC] delegates for their input. Next, MMA's CEO detailed his groups' cooperative agendas. Other speakers pointed to the success of CAL, CAM, HOIM, and NYCCMC.

"From its early work in the USSR to TAP to today's MDS teams, MCC itself provides the finest example of cooperative work," a PDC (MB) delegate said. As an MD who had served with MCC in ROC (i.e., Taiwan) and more recently with CEE in the PRC, he saw cooperation in action. (CEE is supported by MBM/S, COM, EMBMC (now EMM), MBM, NACMC, MCC, MHS, and MMA [ed. note: Mennonite Medical Association, not Mennonite Mutual Aid]). As an NGO, MCC has also cooperated in overseas settings with UN groups such as WHO.

"Could COM, MBM, MBM/S, RMM, and EMBMC work together more effectively?" queried another participant. "Look at AIMM" (formerly CIM), a second delegate responded, pointing to AIMM's EMC, EMCC, EMMC, FEBC (formerly EMB), GC, and MBM/S base of support. An EMBMC YES man agreed.

An MB BCL spokesperson mentioned inter-Mennonite cooperation in publishing by pointing to *ME*,V and the MEA books. "MYW is also inter-Mennonite," a MCEC delegate noted, "as is the LIFE program."

A MBBC student asked for other examples of successful cooperation. Don't forget the work of former AMBS professors J.C. and C.J., one PhD in the room responded. "They brought MBE's GBS and the GC's MBS together—which was no small task." A MHS member noted that, for a time, H.S.'s AV had created an academic unity among MCs and GCs.

But what of broader cooperation and identity among HPCs generally, a BIC VSer from PA wondered. "An HPC i.d. is important," an older man replied. As a WW2 IV-E (i.e., CO) and CPS participant, he applauded new HPC initiatives (e.g., NCP and CPTs). "Those who served in CPS or ASW or 1-W or PAX know the benefits of cooperation," he assured the group.

An EMC professor [ed. note: MBE's EMC&S, not the denominations EMC or EMCC] called for more inter-Mennonite support of church colleges.

However, a MEDA spokesperson KOed the idea of naming specific institutions in any document. "We have to reach out to every one," she said, "the MB, the GC, the BIC, etc." A WMSC delegate agreed, "Let's think about the broader picture—don't forget MWC."

"OK, OK," one CMC representative finally said. "What have I been hearing you all say? I need something to take back to CMBC for input, study, reflection, dialogue, processing, and sharing."

"Let's not be too technical," an MC from DC said. "We need something which will connect with the MYF, not just the MDiv. crowd."

The meeting's m.c. closed the conference at 5 pm, EST.

A listening committee composed of persons from AAMA, MCC-US, GCMC's CDC, and RBI will prepare a final report to be edited by IMS and printed by MPH. MC members may obtain a summary copy ASAP by sending a SASE to MBCM.

Top Ten Names for the New Denomination Created by the MC/GC Merger

10. Anabaptists Anonymous

9. The Non-Amish

8. The New Denomination Created by the Merger

7. Hazel's People

6. The Bigger and Better Mennonite Church

5. Mennonite Church (Anderson, Indiana)

4. Larry

3. One Holy Catholic and Apostolic Mennonite Church

2. A.C.R.O.N.Y.M [Any Creed Received, Only Now You're Mennonite]

1. Troyers "Я" Us

Mennonite Central Committee logo, showing cross and dove

Map of Texas, showing Brownsville

Mennonite Trading Cards

In years past, most Mennonites were related to one another by birth or marriage. Today that is less often the case; however, personal connections are still a must for any Mennonite. Since Warkentin and Gingerich's *Who's Who Among the Mennonites* (1937, 1943) is now somewhat out of date, we've decided to provide you, the New Mennonite, with a brief and updated Who's Who to help you improve your name-dropping skills.

Following in the fine tradition of kids' breakfast cereal gimmicks, we're proud to introduce a brand new line of Mennonite Trading Cards. Clip and save these handy cards and keep them in your wallet, datebook, cookbook, or other quick reference spot. Study your cards carefully and you'll be ready to engage in intelligent-sounding conversation with nearly anyone at a major Mennonite gathering.

Collect all six hundred and six cards!! Trade them with members of your small group!! Educational and fun for the whole family!! Learning about your church has never been so easy!!

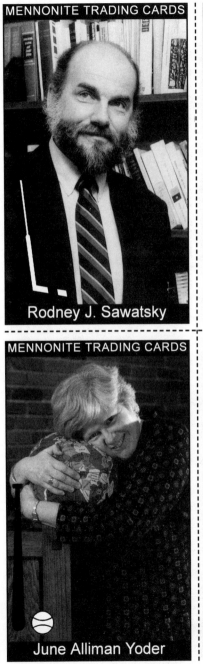

MENNONITE TRADING CARDS

Rodney J. Sawatsky

MENNONITE TRADING CARDS

Anabaptist Collector Series

Menno Simons

MENNONITE TRADING CARDS

June Alliman Yoder

MENNONITE TRADING CARDS

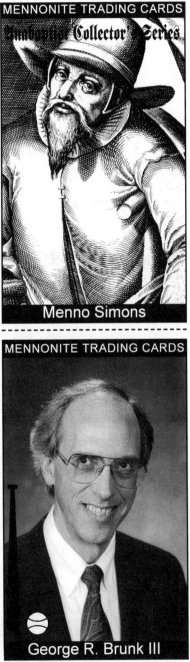

George R. Brunk III

MENNONITE TRADING CARDS

Menno Simons

born: c. 1496   died: 1561
ordained: 1524 (Roman Catholic); 1537 (Anabaptist)
married: Gertrude   home: no permanent address

CAREER HIGHLIGHTS: Served as a parish priest (1524-1536); Anabaptist leader (1536-1561). Wrote several books and tracts. In 1545 north German Anabaptists were first referred to as "Mennisten."

INSIDER TIP FOR THE NEW MENNONITE: Don't be fooled . . . although Mennonites make frequent and laudatory references to Menno, and occasionally even own his *Complete Writings*, in fact, virtually no Mennonite living today has ever read anything Menno wrote.

MENNONITE TRADING CARDS

Rodney J. Sawatsky

born: 1943   married: Lorna Ewert
home: Waterloo, Ontario

COLLEGE CAREER HIGHLIGHT: Ph.D. in church history from Princeton.

LEAGUE CAREER HIGHLIGHTS: Taught Mennonite history at Canadian Mennonite Bible College; Dean, then President (1988-present) of Conrad Grebel College.

The most popular course Sawatsky teaches is "Sects and Cults." This is likely due to young adults having a strong interest in anything which sounds like "sects."

MENNONITE TRADING CARDS

George R. Brunk III

born: 1939   married: Erma Hess
ordained: 1963   home: Harrisonburg, VA

MAJOR LEAGUE CAREER HIGHLIGHTS: Missionary in Italy (1964-1970); Professor at Eastern Mennonite Seminary (1974-present); Dean since 1979; Moderator of the Mennonite Church (1990-1991).

MENNONITE GAME TIP: It is estimated that George is closely related to 54.7% of all ordained persons in the Mennonite Church (both living and deceased). If you suspect that he's related to your pastor or former pastor, you're probably right.

MENNONITE TRADING CARDS

June Alliman Yoder

born: 1944   married: John D. Yoder
ordained: 1988   home: Goshen, IN

MAJOR LEAGUE CAREER HIGHLIGHTS: Professor of communication and preaching (1968-1970, 1981-present); Director of college admissions (1977-1981). Well-known speaker, preacher, and humorist.

INSIDER'S TIP: June is often referred to as the "Mennonite Erma Bombeck."

MENNONITE TRADING CARDS

TEAM CARD

Associated Mennonite
Biblical Seminaries

MENNONITE TRADING CARDS

Hall of Famer

Harold S. Bender

MENNONITE TRADING CARDS

Katie Funk Wiebe

MENNONITE TRADING CARDS

Wally Kroeker

MENNONITE TRADING CARDS

Wally Kroeker

born: May, 1946—"the very first baby-boomer"
married: Millie Loewen   home: Winnipeg, Manitoba
college experience: Fresno Pacific

COLLEGE CAREER HIGHLIGHT: "In 1964-65, when I was both a motorcycle bum and student at Fresno Pacific College, I was notorious for talking in my sleep. The other guys in the dorm sometimes tried to get me to talk. Apparently I got up one night, pulled on my boots and took my Triumph 650 for a ride down Kings Canyon Street, pajamas flapping in the wind. I, of course, remember none of it, as I was sleeping at the time."

LEAGUE CAREER HIGHLIGHTS: Editor, *Christian Leader; The Marketplace* (1985-present)

MENNONITE TRADING CARDS

Harold S. Bender

born: 1897   died: 1962
ordained: 1944   married: Elizabeth Horsch
home: Goshen, IN

MAJOR LEAGUE CAREER HIGHLIGHTS: historian, author, professor, seminary dean (1944-1962); President of Mennonite World Conference (1952-1962); co-editor, *Mennonite Encyclopedia*, vols. 1-4.

MENNONITE GAME FACT: Contrary to popular opinion, Bender's first name was not "Dean."

MENNONITE TRADING CARDS

Katie Funk Wiebe

born: 1924   home playing field: Wichita, KS

MAJOR LEAGUE CAREER HIGHLIGHTS: Author/editor of a dozen books and hundreds of articles; columnist; professor at Tabor College, Hillsboro, KS, 1967-1990.

FUN FACT: Snow princess at 1941 ice carnival at hometown in northern Saskatchewan. Costume: floor-length crepe paper dress over ski suit.

MENNONITE TRADING CARDS

Associated Mennonite Biblical Seminaries

home field: Elkhart, IN
manager: Marlin E. Miller
team captain: Gayle Gerber Koontz
head coach: Richard A. Kauffman

TEAM HIGHLIGHTS: As part of the deal which took the Brooklyn Dodgers to Los Angeles, two Mennonite seminaries—one in Chicago, IL, and another in Goshen, IN—merged their starting rosters in 1958. The teams' front office management integrated in 1990.

MENNONITE TRADING CARDS

Willard M. Swartley

MENNONITE TRADING CARDS

Anabaptist Collector's Series

COMPOSITE SKETCH

Uli Seiler

MENNONITE TRADING CARDS

Myron S. Augsburger

MENNONITE TRADING CARDS

Merle Good & Phyllis
Pellman Good

MENNONITE TRADING CARDS

Uli Seiler

born and died: unknown
occupation: peasant

home: Grueningen, Switzerland

Better known as: "Bad Uli," or "The Anabaptist With One Hand."

REFORMATION ACTIVITIES: One of the first Anabaptists in Grueningen; led a prison breakout in February 1526; known to regularly carry a gun; disrupted state-church services by shooting pigeons from the church bell tower on Sunday mornings while the priest was delivering his sermon inside.

MENNONITE TRADING CARDS

Willard M. Swartley

born: 1936
ordained: 1961

married: Mary Lapp
home: Elkhart, IN

MINOR LEAGUE EXPERIENCE: Fuller Brush Sales Representative

MAJOR LEAGUE CAREER HIGHLIGHTS: Pastor (1961-1965); New Testament teacher (1962 -present)

Willard began his Big League career as a rookie on the '62 Goshen club, but developed into a star with the Harrisonburg team. In 1975 Willard took advantage of the League's free agent option and signed on with the Canadian franchise. He eventually ended up playing in Elkhart.

MENNONITE TRADING CARDS

Merle Good and Phyllis Pellman Good

born: 1946 and 1948

home: Lancaster, PA

MAJOR LEAGUE CAREER HIGHLIGHTS: Since 1969 the Good-n-Good Tag-Team has cooperated on a number of artistic and literary projects in drama, publishing, and film. Projects have included: Dutch Family Festival (1969-1978); Festival Quarterly (since 1974); The People's Place (since 1976); and Good Books (since 1979).

FUN FACTS: Merle helped to set a family muskrat-trapping record. His six brothers had no sisters. Together the seven formed a formidable team in any sport, though "verbalizing" was their favorite game. Phyllis nonviolently terminated flies with sharp knives during her tenure at a farmer's market stand. She fled to the Middle East (with MCC) the summer she promised to marry Merle, but returned on schedule.

MENNONITE TRADING CARDS

Myron S. Augsburger

born: 1929
ordained: 1951

married: Esther Kniss
home: Washington D.C.

MAJOR LEAGUE CAREER HIGHLIGHTS: Evangelist (1955-present); President, Eastern Mennonite College (1965-1980); Moderator of the Mennonite Church (1983-1985); currently, President, Christian College Coalition.

MENNONITE GAME TIP: Myron is the brother of A. Don Augsburger, Sarasota, FL, and David W. Augsburger, Pasadena, CA.

MENNONITE PRONUNCIATION TIP: Many Mennonites pronounce Myron's first name as "Marron."

MENNONITE TRADING CARDS

José Ortíz

MENNONITE TRADING CARDS

Hall of Famer

Frank H. Epp

MENNONITE TRADING CARDS

Phyllis Driver Diller

MENNONITE TRADING CARDS

C. Norman Kraus

MENNONITE TRADING CARDS

C. Norman Kraus

born: 1924
ordained: 1950
married: Ruth Smith
home: Harrisonburg, VA

MAJOR LEAGUE CAREER HIGHLIGHTS: pastor; Bible and religion teacher (1951-1987); author.

After several decades of coaching in North America, Norman and Ruth spent the years 1966-1967 and 1980-1987 working with teams in Asia and the Pacific. He continues to do some occasional relief pitching and pinch-hitting for various Mennonite institutions.

MENNONITE TRADING CARDS

Frank H. Epp

born: 1929
married: Helen Dick
died: 1986
home: Canada!

MAJOR LEAGUE CAREER HIGHLIGHTS: President Conrad Grebel College (1973-1979); parliamentary candidate (1979, 1980); radio speaker (1957-1963); editor and author.

MENNONITE TRADING CARDS

Phyllis Driver Diller

born: 1917, Lima, OH
attended Bluffton (OH) College, 1938-1939

CAREER HIGHLIGHT: Bluffton College commencement speaker, 1993.

MENNONITE TRADING CARDS

José Ortiz

born: May 3 and May 15, 1939
ordained: 1972
married: Iraida Rivera
home: Harrisonburg, VA

MAJOR LEAGUE CAREER HIGHLIGHTS: pastor (1969-1973; 1982-1983); church administrator (1974-1982); Director of Hispanic Ministries Program (1985-1993).

To avoid a fine for late reporting, the midwife who delivered José reported his date of birth to be 12 days later, a date which remains on "official" documents. In more ways than one, José knows, "you must be born again."

Getting to Know
Your Mennonite Periodicals

New Mennonites are frequently baffled by the surprising array of Mennonite-published magazines, newletters, and newspapers. There are literally dozens of Mennonite church papers, each with a slightly different constituency, focus, or slant. While it might well take years to familiarize yourself with the plethora of Mennonite serials now in the mail, a selection appears below which you may want to explore first. Along with each title is a sample headline or article title typical of the publication.

The Mennonite Reporter
(Waterloo, ON; Canadian inter-Mennonite news)—
"Swift Current Mennonite Churches
Wash Away in Torrential Downpour"

The Mennonite
*(Newton, KS; publication of the General Conference
Mennonite Church)—*
"GCs Abandon Integration Plans with MCs; Will Pursue
Merger with GM"

The Mennonite Quarterly Review
(Goshen, IN; historical studies)—
"A Tedious Theological Disputation Between Two Obscure
Anabaptists in the South Tyrol, 1527"

Festival Quarterly
(Intercourse, PA; Mennonite art and culture)—
"Please Accept Me!: Promoting the Artist Inside Me"

Mennonite Weekly Review
(Newton, KS; U. S. inter-Mennonite news)—
"Wayland, Iowa, Mennonite Softball Player Hits Grand Slam;
Is Able to Touch Base With Three of His Teammates"

Christian Leader
(Hillsboro, KS; publication of U.S. Mennonite Brethren)—
"Lester and Lydia Buller of Freeman, S.D. Wed Fifty Years
This Month; Lydia Releases Her Memoirs Entitled
'Living More With Les'"

Gospel Herald
(Scottdale, PA; publication of the Mennonite Church)—
"Moderator Describes Grueling General Board Meeting:
'We Were Processing Like Vegetables'"

The Sword and Trumpet
(Harrisonburg, VA; conservative Mennonite thought)—
"Preparing Doctrinally for the Last Judgment"

Mennonite Central Committee Peace
Section Washington Memo
(Akron, PA; peace interests news)—
"Washington Office Staff Member Forced to Resign After
Admitting She Is a Registered Republican"

Family Life
(Aylmer, ON; Old Order Amish and Mennonite magazine)—
"*Gelassenheit* Versus *Fahrvergnuegen:*
The Church and the Automobile Today"

Institutions Quiz

1. Men who apply for admission to a Mennonite
   seminary must agree to
   a) attend classes regularly.
   b) uphold Mennonite doctrine.
   c) grow facial hair.

2. Frequent mailings by church agencies greatly
   facilitate
   a) congregational awareness.
   b) inter-Mennonite communication.
   c) the destruction of forests.

3. In breaking with the authority of Rome, Mennonites
   have come to favor
   a) servant leadership.
   b) the priesthood of all believers.
   c) Elkhart.

4. Mennonites who feel out of step with their
   congregations
   a) unite for change.
   b) join the Methodists.
   c) apply to AMBS.

5. Anabaptist writings are tucked away and forgotten in
   a) European museums.
   b) American farmhouse attics.
   c) Provident Bookstores.

6. At church-wide conventions, "606" refers to
   a) the number of the closing hymn.
   b) the room number at your hotel.
   c) the time people begin arriving for the 6 a.m. prayer
      meeting.

7. Mennonite parents send their children to church
   colleges to get
   a) a quality education.
   b) familiarity with the Mennonite world.
   c) a Mennonite spouse.

8. Mennonites under age 30 give generous
   contributions to
   a) MCC.
   b) MDS.
   c) NPR.

9. Mennonite scholars see frequent references to their
   books in the pages of
   a) *Conrad Grebel Review.*
   b) *The Mennonite Quarterly Review.*
   c) *The Sword and Trumpet.*

10. Mennonites deal with the proliferation of
    committees by
    a) eliminating obsolete tasks.
    b) merging several committees into one.
    c) forming a task force to study the issues and report on
       possible solutions.

The publication of
The Mennonite Starter Kit
illustrates that:

a) Mennonites have a good sense of humor.

b) Good Books is an imaginative publishing company.

c) anyone can write a book.

An Abundance of Good Books

The Country Stain Quilt
by G. Wiebe-Friesen

If you can't have a house in the country, at least you can have the country in your house! This new book gives you 3 pattern variations to choose from:

Grandad's Footprints
Tractor Oil
and Barnyard Memories
(also available in
scratch-and-sniff)

Excellent for beginners!

Three Mennonite Poets and a Baby
by Ted Janzen, Tom Sell and Steve Good-Bergey
Edited by Vera Nyce-Reimer

For those who thought the original **Three Mennonite Poets** wasn't very cute, we've added a baby! Three new poets under the editorial supervision of Vera Nyce-Reimer have produced a collection which stands in the tradition of inspirational Mennonite singsong poetry. We guarantee a tear and a smile.

Nyce-Reimer's daughter Emma is featured in the illustrations.

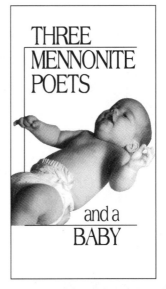

THREE
MENNONITE
POETS

and a
BABY

Good Books

Intercourse, PA 17534

The Authors

MENNONITE TRADING CARDS — Steve Nolt

MENNONITE TRADING CARDS — Craig Haas

TRADING TIP: Any six of these author cards can be traded at even value for any other Mennonite Trading cards in this book.

MENNONITE TRADING CARDS

Craig Haas

born: 1956
home: Manheim, PA

married: Chris

MINOR LEAGUE EXPERIENCE: Graduated from Millersville University (1980) and the University of Chicago (1982) with degrees in Philosophy. (These institutions must be really "proud" of *this* book.)

MAJOR LEAGUE CAREER HIGHLIGHTS: Church planter and pastor; currently employed by The People's Place, Intercourse, PA; teaches part-time at the Lancaster campus of Harrisburg Area Community College. His book *Readings from Mennonite Writings, New and Old* was published by Good Books in 1992.

Craig was once a New Mennonite himself. Today his greatest fear is that some reviewer will describe something he wrote as "a good read."

MENNONITE TRADING CARDS

Steve Nolt

born: 1968
home: Elkhart, IN ("The City with a Heart")

married: Rachel

MINOR LEAGUE EXPERIENCE: History student, graduate of Goshen College (A.D. 1990); seminary student.

MAJOR LEAGUE CAREER HIGHLIGHTS: Numerous serious articles in the field of Mennonite history, and the book *A History of the Amish*, published by Good Books in 1992. Steve was recently returned to the minors, to the AMBS farm team.

Steve was once asked to appear on stage as Elvis Presley, due to his striking physical resemblance to the King of Rock and Roll.